STATE PROFILES

MASSACHUSETTS

BY NATHAN SOMMER

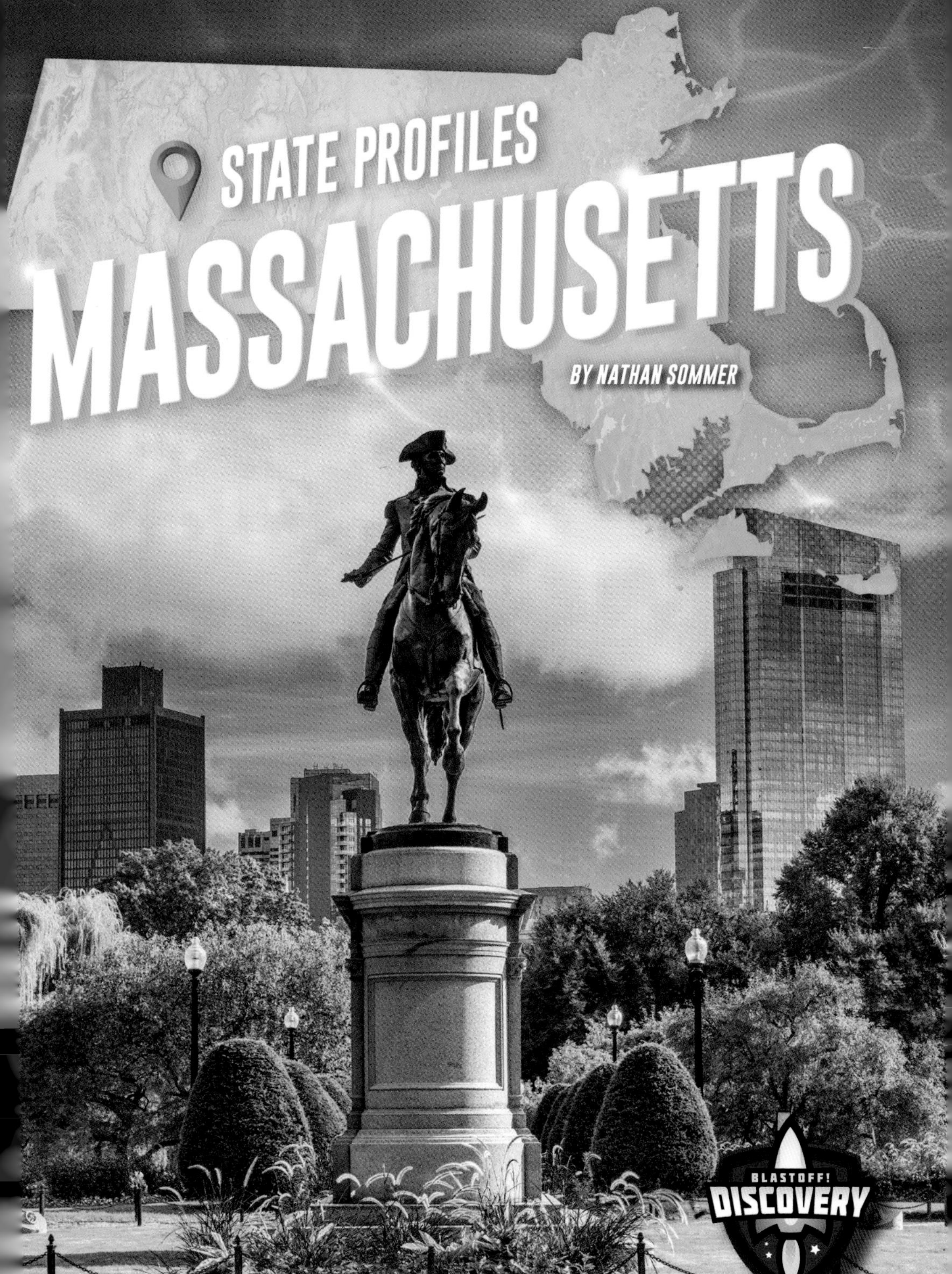

BELLWETHER MEDIA • MINNEAPOLIS, MN

BLASTOFF!
DISCOVERY

Blastoff! Discovery launches a new mission: reading to learn. Filled with facts and features, each book offers you an exciting new world to explore!

This edition first published in 2022 by Bellwether Media, Inc.

No part of this publication may be reproduced in whole or in part without written permission of the publisher.
For information regarding permission, write to Bellwether Media, Inc., Attention: Permissions Department,
6012 Blue Circle Drive, Minnetonka, MN 55343.

Library of Congress Cataloging-in-Publication Data

Names: Sommer, Nathan, author.
Title: Massachusetts / Nathan Sommer.
Description: Minneapolis, MN : Bellwether Media, 2022. |
    Series: Blastoff! Discovery: State profiles | Includes bibliographical
    references and index. | Audience: Ages 7-13 | Audience: Grades
    4-6 | Summary: "Engaging images accompany information about
    Massachusetts. The combination of high-interest subject matter and
    narrative text is intended for students in grades 3 through 8"
    – Provided by publisher.
Identifiers: LCCN 2021019643 (print) | LCCN 2021019644 (ebook)
    | ISBN 9781644873922 (library binding) |
    ISBN 9781648341694 (ebook)
Subjects: LCSH: Massachusetts–Juvenile literature.
Classification: LCC F64.3 .S66 2022 (print) | LCC F64.3 (ebook) |
    DDC 974.4–dc23
LC record available at https://lccn.loc.gov/2021019643
LC ebook record available at https://lccn.loc.gov/2021019644

Editor: Colleen Sexton   Designer: Laura Sowers

Printed in the United States of America, North Mankato, MN.

TABLE OF CONTENTS

BUNKER HILL

It is a summer day in Boston. A tour guide leads a group along the Freedom Trail. This path through the city tells the story of the **American Revolution**. The group's first stop is the Old South Meeting House. The guide explains how **colonists** gathered there to plan the Boston Tea Party.

THE USS CONSTITUTION

The USS *Constitution* is the world's oldest military ship still afloat. Built in 1794, it actively sailed the seas until the 1930s!

CAPE COD NATIONAL SEASHORE

MINUTE MAN NATIONAL HISTORICAL PARK

PLYMOUTH ROCK

SALEM WITCH MUSEUM

Later, the group boards the USS *Constitution*. This historic ship fought at sea more than 200 years ago. The Freedom Trail ends at Bunker Hill. A monument tells about the battle fought there. The group is amazed by how much history the city holds. Welcome to Massachusetts!

Massachusetts is part of **New England**. The state covers 10,554 square miles (27,335 square kilometers) in the northeastern United States. It touches New Hampshire and Vermont to the north. The state shares its western border with New York. Connecticut and Rhode Island lie to the south. Eastern Massachusetts juts into the Atlantic Ocean.

Massachusetts is known as the Bay State. Cape Cod Bay and Buzzards Bay help shape the state's curved **peninsula**. Martha's Vineyard and Nantucket are islands that lie off the southeastern coast. The capital city of Boston sits on the Atlantic coast. Other major cities include Worcester and Springfield.

VERMONT

NEW YORK

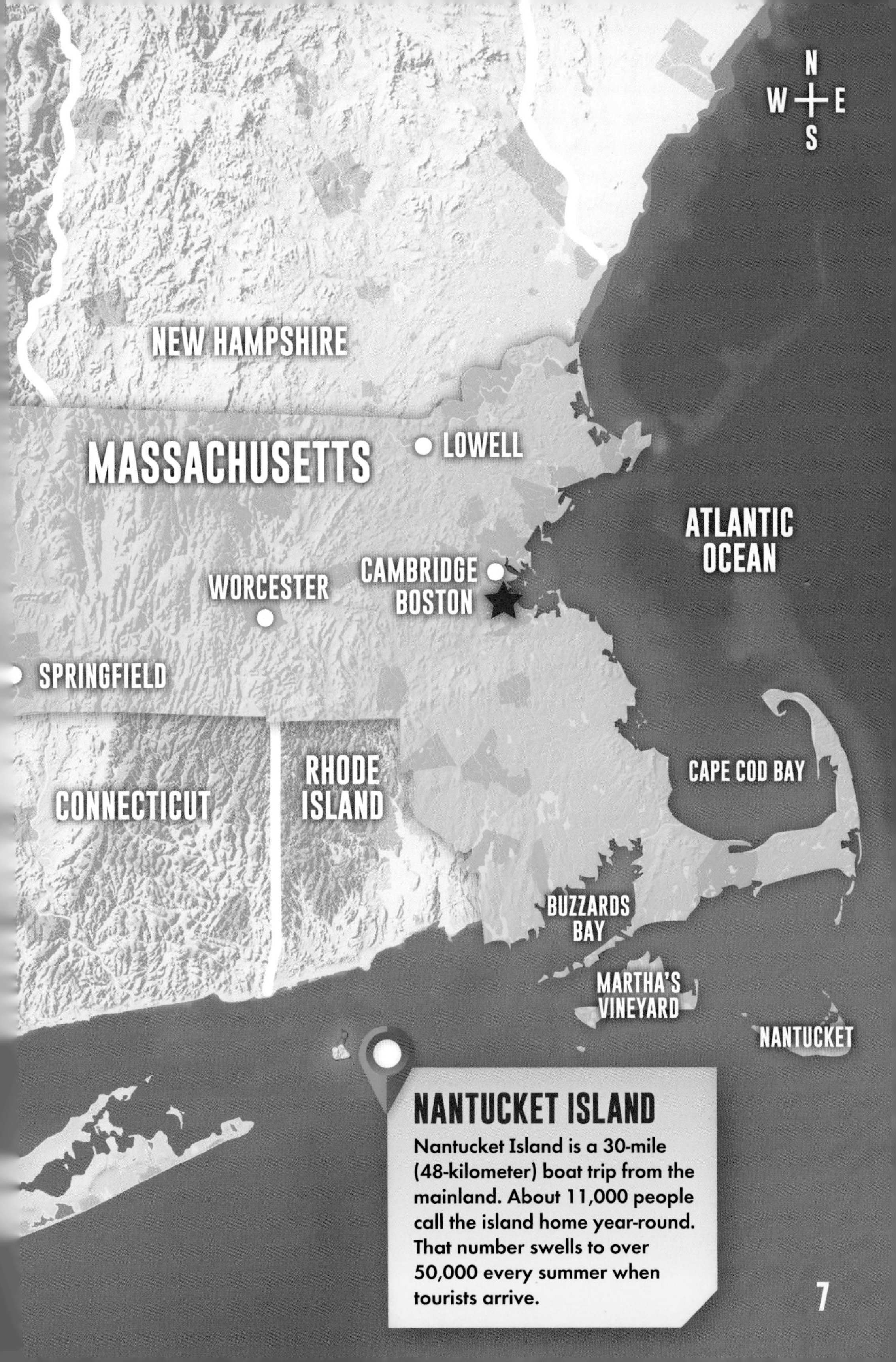

N
W E
S

NEW HAMPSHIRE

MASSACHUSETTS

LOWELL

ATLANTIC
OCEAN

CAMBRIDGE
WORCESTER   BOSTON

SPRINGFIELD

RHODE
ISLAND

CAPE COD BAY

CONNECTICUT

BUZZARDS
BAY

MARTHA'S
VINEYARD

NANTUCKET

NANTUCKET ISLAND

Nantucket Island is a 30-mile
(48-kilometer) boat trip from the
mainland. About 11,000 people
call the island home year-round.
That number swells to over
50,000 every summer when
tourists arrive.

7

PILGRIMS LANDING
PLYMOUTH

People first arrived in Massachusetts about 10,000 years ago. In time, they formed Native American tribes. These groups included the Wampanoag, Nipmuc, Pocumtuc, and Massachusett. In 1620, the *Mayflower* brought Pilgrims from England to settle Plymouth. The Wampanoag taught the Pilgrims how to grow food to survive. In 1630, **Puritans** arrived from England to form the Massachusetts Bay Colony.

THE BOSTON TEA PARTY

In 1773, colonists in Boston dumped 342 chests of tea into Boston Harbor. They were protesting a British tax on the tea. Britain responded with harsh new laws. These laws united the colonists to fight for their freedom.

Massachusetts became 1 of 13 English colonies. The colonies fought the **Revolutionary War** for their independence. The war's first shots were fired at Lexington and Concord in Massachusetts. In 1788, Massachusetts became the sixth state to sign the U.S. **Constitution**.

NATIVE PEOPLES OF MASSACHUSETTS

MASHPEE WAMPANOAG TRIBE

- Original Wampanoag lands in southeastern Massachusetts and eastern Rhode Island
- About 2,600 in Massachusetts today

WAMPANOAG TRIBE OF AQUINNAH

- Original Wampanoag lands in southeastern Massachusetts and eastern Rhode Island
- Traditional Aquinnah land on Noepe Island (also known as Martha's Vineyard)
- More than 900 members in Massachusetts today with about 300 on Noepe Island

Coastal lowlands cover eastern Massachusetts. The state's long coastline features beautiful harbors. Low hills, swamps, and lakes lie inland. Central Massachusetts features rounded hills on a low **plateau**. The Connecticut River cuts through the region. The land rises to the Berkshire Hills in the west. The Berkshire Valley lies between these hills. The Taconic Mountains are farther west. Mount Greylock stands in the northwest. It is the state's highest point.

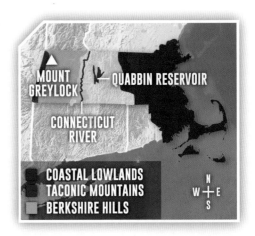

MOUNT GREYLOCK

QUABBIN RESERVOIR

CONNECTICUT RIVER

COASTAL LOWLANDS
TACONIC MOUNTAINS
BERKSHIRE HILLS

N
W＋E
S

CAPE COD

THE QUABBIN RESERVOIR

The Quabbin Reservoir in central Massachusetts is the state's largest body of water. This lake covers 39 square miles (101 square kilometers). It is the main water supply for Boston and other communities.

QUABBIN RESERVOIR

SPRING
HIGH: 56°F (13°C)
LOW: 38°F (3°C)

SUMMER
HIGH: 79°F (26°C)
LOW: 61°F (16°C)

FALL
HIGH: 60°F (16°C)
LOW: 44°F (7°C)

WINTER
HIGH: 37°F (3°C)
LOW: 22°F (-6°C)

°F = degrees Fahrenheit
°C = degrees Celsius

Massachusetts experiences all four seasons. It has warm, rainy summers and cold, snowy winters. **Nor'easters** can bring heavy snow in winter.

Deer, raccoons, and opossums roam Massachusetts's forests. They dodge attacks from bobcats and coyotes. Black bears and moose also wander these woodlands. Largemouth bass, crappies, and sunfish swim in the state's lakes and rivers. Snapping turtles and eastern ribbon snakes lurk near wetlands.

Sandpipers and piping plovers fly along the Massachusetts coast. There, great blue herons feast on blue crabs, scup, and striped bass. Humpback whales swim in the state's bays. They share these waters with around 400 **endangered** right whales. Young sea turtles spend summers in the bays. Stingrays hide in deep waters offshore.

GREAT BLUE HERON

MOOSE

ROUGHTAIL STINGRAY

PIPING PLOVER

SNAPPING TURTLE

FRIENDLY GIANTS

FRIENDLY GIANTS

Stellwagen Bank National Marine Sanctuary is one the world's top whale-watching locations. The humpbacks there are gentle toward visitors. They often jump out of the water!

HUMPBACK WHALE

Life Span: up to 95 years
Status: least concern

humpback whale range = ■

LEAST CONCERN	NEAR THREATENED	VULNERABLE	ENDANGERED	CRITICALLY ENDANGERED	EXTINCT IN THE WILD	EXTINCT
▲						

More than 7 million people call Massachusetts home. They are called Bay Staters. The state's population is mostly **urban**. Nearly 4.9 million people live in and around Boston. Western Massachusetts is mostly **rural**. Residents live on farms and in small towns.

MASSACHUSETTS'S CHALLENGE: RURAL SCHOOLS

Rural schools are receiving less funding as the number of students drops. Now these schools cannot afford the teachers and technology they need. The state must work to make education equal for all students.

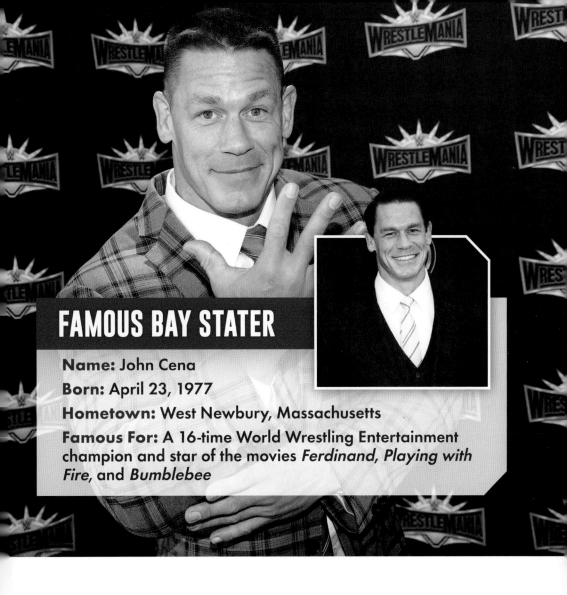

FAMOUS BAY STATER

Name: John Cena
Born: April 23, 1977
Hometown: West Newbury, Massachusetts
Famous For: A 16-time World Wrestling Entertainment champion and star of the movies *Ferdinand, Playing with Fire,* and *Bumblebee*

Around 7 in 10 Bay Staters have European **ancestors**. Many came from Ireland, Italy, and England. Hispanic Americans and Black or African Americans each make up about one-tenth of the population. Smaller numbers of Asian Americans and Native Americans live in the state. Recent **immigrants** hail from China, the Dominican Republic, Brazil, India, and Haiti.

Boston is one of the country's oldest cities. It was founded in 1630 by Puritan colonists. In 1632, it became Massachusetts's capital. Boston's location made it a busy seaport. Today, Boston is the state's largest city. Historic buildings mix with skyscrapers.

Boston is a world leader in education. Harvard University, Boston College, and the Massachusetts Institute of Technology are in the area. Boston is also a center for the arts. Residents enjoy the Boston Pops Orchestra and the Museum of Fine Arts. Locals stroll through Boston Common, the country's first public park. People head to the Faneuil Hall Marketplace for food and shopping.

GOING UNDERGROUND

The Ted Williams Tunnel is North America's deepest tunnel. It sends drivers 90 feet (27 meters) beneath Boston Harbor.

BOSTON COMMON

CRANBERRY BOG

Massachusetts's early **settlers** depended on farming and fishing. Today, farmland covers about one-tenth of the state. Farmers grow cranberries, apples, and sweet corn. They also raise dairy cows and turkeys. Massachusetts is a leading fishing state. Crews haul in scallops, lobsters, and cod.

MASSACHUSETTS'S CHALLENGE: THE FISHING INDUSTRY

New England has some of the fastest-warming waters in the world due to climate change. It is harder for lobsters, scallops, and fish to survive. That means the catch is getting smaller. There are also fewer jobs available on fishing crews.

Manufacturing became a major industry in the 1800s. Immigrants found work in factories making cloth, shoes, and tools. Today, factory workers produce computer parts, electronic equipment, and medicines. Most Bay Staters have **service jobs**. They work in hospitals, banks, and schools. The state's booming **tourism** industry employs workers in hotels and museums.

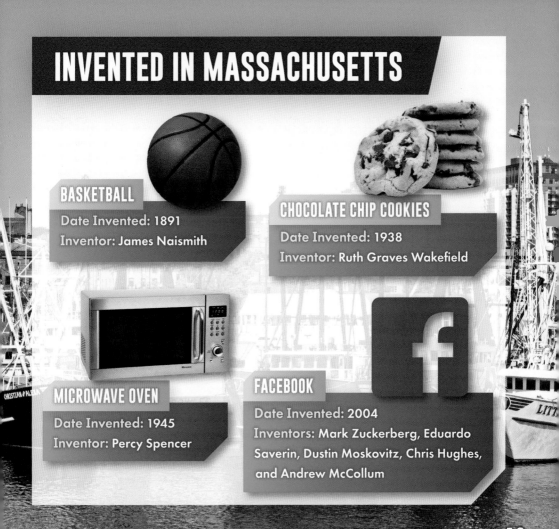

INVENTED IN MASSACHUSETTS

BASKETBALL
Date Invented: 1891
Inventor: James Naismith

CHOCOLATE CHIP COOKIES
Date Invented: 1938
Inventor: Ruth Graves Wakefield

MICROWAVE OVEN
Date Invented: 1945
Inventor: Percy Spencer

FACEBOOK
Date Invented: 2004
Inventors: Mark Zuckerberg, Eduardo Saverin, Dustin Moskovitz, Chris Hughes, and Andrew McCollum

CLAMBAKE

Bay Staters enjoy fresh seafood. Fried clams and seared scallops appear on menus statewide. Clam chowder mixes clams, onions, potatoes, and cream into a hearty soup. Cooks serve lobster rolls hot with butter or cold with mayonnaise. For clambakes, people steam clams, lobster, corn, and red potatoes over a fire.

LOBSTER ROLL

Boston earned the nickname Beantown for its famous baked beans. This side dish stews navy beans with molasses and bacon. Boston has its own dessert, too. Boston cream pie is a custard-filled yellow cake covered in chocolate. In the fall, Bay Staters enjoy cider doughnuts. Cinnamon and sugar cover these apple-flavored treats.

SANDWICHES FOR DESSERT?

The fluffernutter is a popular New England dessert invented in Massachusetts. This sandwich features marshmallow creme and peanut butter between slices of white bread.

BOSTON CREAM PIE

8 SERVINGS

Have an adult help you make this sweet treat!

INGREDIENTS

1 box yellow cake mix and the ingredients listed in the instructions on the box

1 box vanilla pudding mix

2 3/4 cups of milk

16 ounces of hot fudge topping

maraschino cherries

DIRECTIONS

1. Heat the oven to 350 degrees Fahrenheit (177 degrees Celsius).

2. Follow the instructions on the box to mix the cake batter.

3. Pour the batter into two round cake pans. Follow the instructions on the box to bake them.

4. Combine the pudding and milk in a mixing bowl and beat on low speed for 2 to 3 minutes. Cover the bowl and put it in the refrigerator for 30 minutes.

5. Remove the cooled cakes from the pans. Spread the chilled pudding mix on one cake. Add the other cake on top to make a two-layer cake.

6. Warm the hot fudge topping and spread it on the cake. Top with maraschino cherries.

7. Let the fudge topping cool. Cut the cake into slices and enjoy!

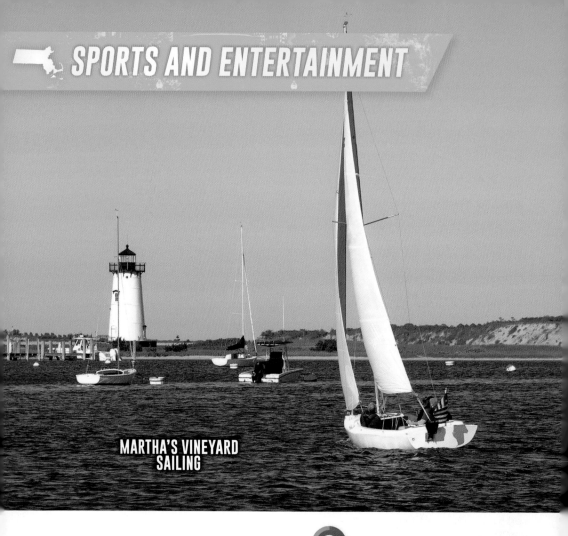

MARTHA'S VINEYARD SAILING

Bay Staters get outside year-round. Skiers head to the Berkshire Hills in winter. This area is also a popular place to view fall colors. Nantucket and Martha's Vineyard offer sailing and fishing. Hikers enjoy ocean views on their way to Nantucket's Great Point Lighthouse.

MAKING MUSIC

The Boston Symphony Orchestra is known as one of the world's best. The musicians play to thousands of fans each year in the historic Symphony Hall.

The Boston Children's Museum provides hands-on fun for kids. Visitors watch thousands of ocean animals at the New England Aquarium. Sports fans cheer on Patriots football, Bruins hockey, and Revolution soccer. Crowds also fill the stands for Celtics basketball games. Fans take in Red Sox baseball games at historic Fenway Park.

NEW ENGLAND AQUARIUM

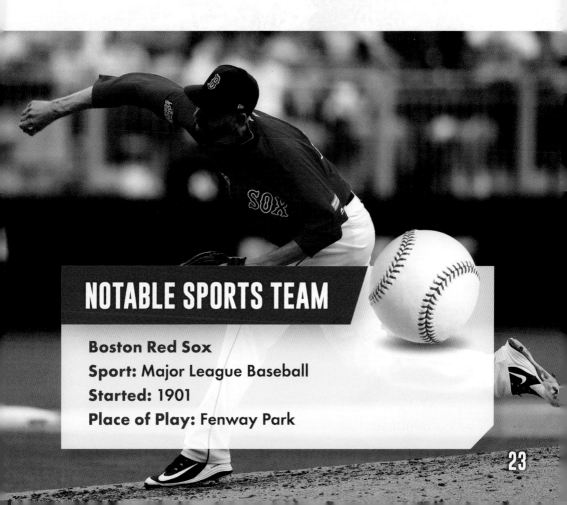

NOTABLE SPORTS TEAM

Boston Red Sox
Sport: Major League Baseball
Started: 1901
Place of Play: Fenway Park

GREASY POLE CONTEST
SAINT PETER'S FIESTA

Festivals bring Bay Staters together. Around one million people crowd the streets for Boston's Saint Patrick's Day parade. The Italian community celebrates Saint Peter's Fiesta in Gloucester each June. This festival features the Greasy Pole Contest. Competitors must cross a long, slippery pole without plunging into the water below!

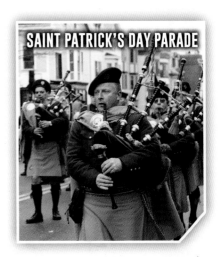

SAINT PATRICK'S DAY PARADE

Each summer, the Tanglewood Music Festival in the Berkshire Hills showcases all types of music. The Jacob's Pillow Dance Festival in Becket features ballet, ballroom, and hip-hop dancing. In April, **reenactments** of the Battles of Lexington and Concord draw big crowds. Bay Staters are proud to carry on Massachusetts's rich history!

THE OLDEST MARATHON

Boston is home to the world's oldest marathon. The event started with 15 runners in 1897. Today, the Boston Marathon draws thousands of athletes from all over the world.

BATTLE OF LEXINGTON REENACTMENT

1630

Puritan settlers from England form the Massachusetts Bay Colony

1773

Objecting to the British tea tax, colonists dump tea from a ship into Boston Harbor, an event known as the Boston Tea Party

PRE-1600S

Native American groups, including the Wampanoag, Nipmuc, and Massachusett, live in what is now Massachusetts

1620

The *Mayflower*, carrying the Pilgrims, arrives in Plymouth

1775

The first shots in the Revolutionary War are fired at Lexington and Concord

1788

Massachusetts becomes the sixth state

1974

White students are bused to Black schools and Black students are bused to white schools to desegregate schools across Massachusetts

1876

In Boston, Alexander Graham Bell makes the first telephone call

2013

Two bombs explode at the finish line of the Boston Marathon

2004

The Boston Red Sox win the World Series, ending the 86-year stretch since their last championship

1960

Massachusetts native John F. Kennedy is elected the 35th president of the United States

Nicknames: The Bay State, The Pilgrim State, The Old Colony State

Motto: *Ense Petit Placidam sub Libertate Quietem* (By the Sword We Seek Peace, But Peace Only Under Liberty)

Date of Statehood: February 6, 1788 (the 6th state)

Capital City: Boston ★

Other Major Cities: Worcester, Springfield, Lowell, Cambridge

Area: 10,554 square miles (27,335 square kilometers); Massachusetts is the 44th largest state.

Population

7,029,917

(2020)

STATE FLAG

Adopted in 1908, Massachusetts's flag is white with a blue shield featuring a Native American. The man holds a bow in his right hand and an arrow in his left. The arrow points down, meaning he is peaceful. The white star on the shield symbolizes that Massachusetts was one of the original 13 states. An arm holding a sword above the shield represents the state motto. The motto is on a ribbon around the shield. Lawmakers are working on a new design to better represent all people in the state.

INDUSTRY

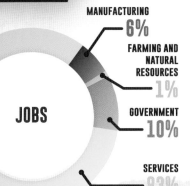

JOBS

MANUFACTURING
6%

FARMING AND NATURAL RESOURCES
1%

GOVERNMENT
10%

SERVICES
83%

Main Exports

machinery

gold

aircraft

natural gas

medical parts

Natural Resources
gold, natural gas, sand, gravel

GOVERNMENT

11 ELECTORAL VOTES

Federal Government

9 | 2
REPRESENTATIVES | SENATORS

USA

MA

State Government

160 | 40
REPRESENTATIVES | SENATORS

STATE SYMBOLS

STATE BIRD
BLACK-CAPPED CHICKADEE

STATE FISH
COD

STATE FLOWER
MAYFLOWER

STATE TREE
AMERICAN ELM

American Revolution—the time in history when American colonists fought against British rule and formed the United States as a country

ancestors—relatives who lived long ago

colonists—people sent by a government to a new region or territory

constitution—the basic principles and laws of a nation

endangered—at risk of disappearing forever

immigrants—people who move to a new country

manufacturing—a field of work in which people use machines to make products

New England—an area in the northeastern United States that includes Maine, New Hampshire, Vermont, Massachusetts, Rhode Island, and Connecticut

nor'easters—large storms that hit coastal northeastern states; winds blow in from the northeast.

peninsula—a section of land that extends out from a larger piece of land and is almost completely surrounded by water

plateau—an area of flat, raised land

Puritans—a group of Christians that disagreed with the Church of England

reenactments—the acting out of past events

Revolutionary War—the war from 1775 to 1783 in which the United States fought for independence from Great Britain

rural—related to the countryside

service jobs—jobs that perform tasks for people or businesses

settlers—people who move to live in a new, undeveloped region

tourism—the business of people traveling to visit other places

urban—related to cities or city life

TO LEARN MORE

AT THE LIBRARY

Juettner, Carie. *The Ghostly Tales of New England.*
Charleston, S.C.: Arcadia Publishing, 2020.

Panchyk, Richard. *Boston History for Kids: From Red Coats to Red Sox with 21 Activities.* Chicago, Ill.: Chicago Review Press, 2018.

Thompson, Ben. *The American Revolution.*
New York, N.Y.: Little, Brown and Company, 2017.

ON THE WEB

FACTSURFER

Factsurfer.com gives you
a safe, fun way to find
more information.

1. Go to www.factsurfer.com.

2. Enter "Massachusetts" into the search box and click 🔍.

3. Select your book cover to see a list of related content.

INDEX